Frédéric Chopin
(1810–1849)

Sonatas

Sonates

Sonaten

for piano • pour piano • für Klavier

Urtext

K 172

MUSICA PIANO

**OVER 25.000 PAGES OF PIANO
MUSIC SHEETS ONLINE**

Bach, Beethoven, Brahms, Chopin, Czerny,
Debussy, Gershwin, Dvořák, Grieg, Haydn,
Joplin, Lyadov, Mendelssohn-Bartholdy, Mozart,
Mussorgsky, Purcell, Schubert, Schumann,
Scriabin, Tchaikovsky and many more

KÖNEMANN

© 2018 koenemann.com GmbH
www.koenemann.com

Editor: Gábor Csalog
Responsible co-editor: Tamás Zaszkaliczky
Technical editor: Desző Varga
Engraved by Kottamester Bt., Budapest

critical notes available on www.frechmann.com

ISBN 978-3-7419-1437-9

Printed in China by Reliance Printing

K 172

INDEX

Sonate
Op. 4, BI 23 — pag. 4

Sonate
Op. 35, BI 128 — pag. 39

Sonate
Op. 58, BI 155 — pag. 67

Sonate

Op. 4
Brown-Index 23
1828

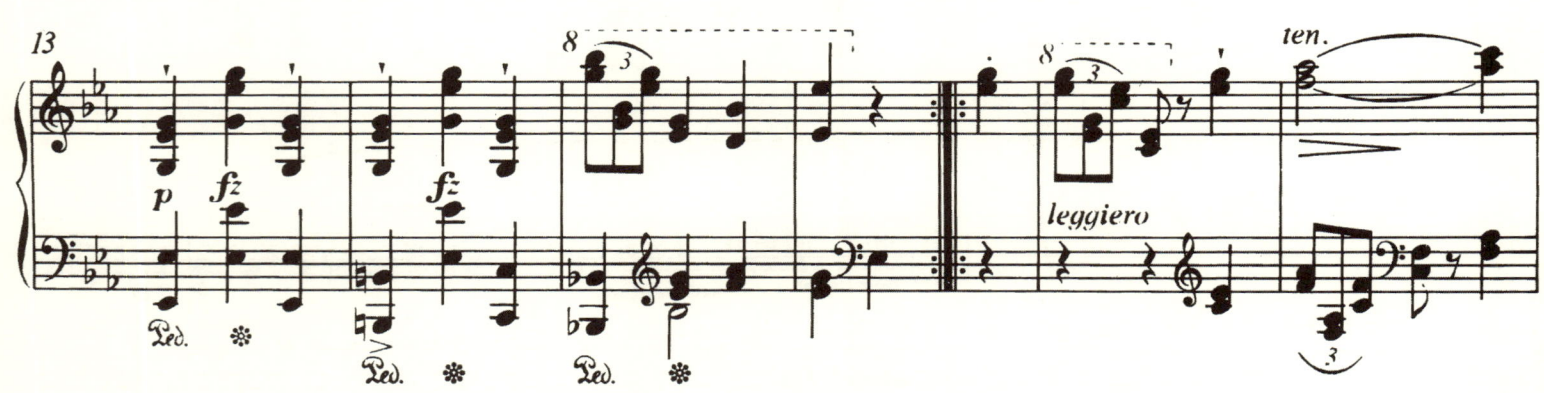

Sonate

Op. 35
Brown-Index 128
1839

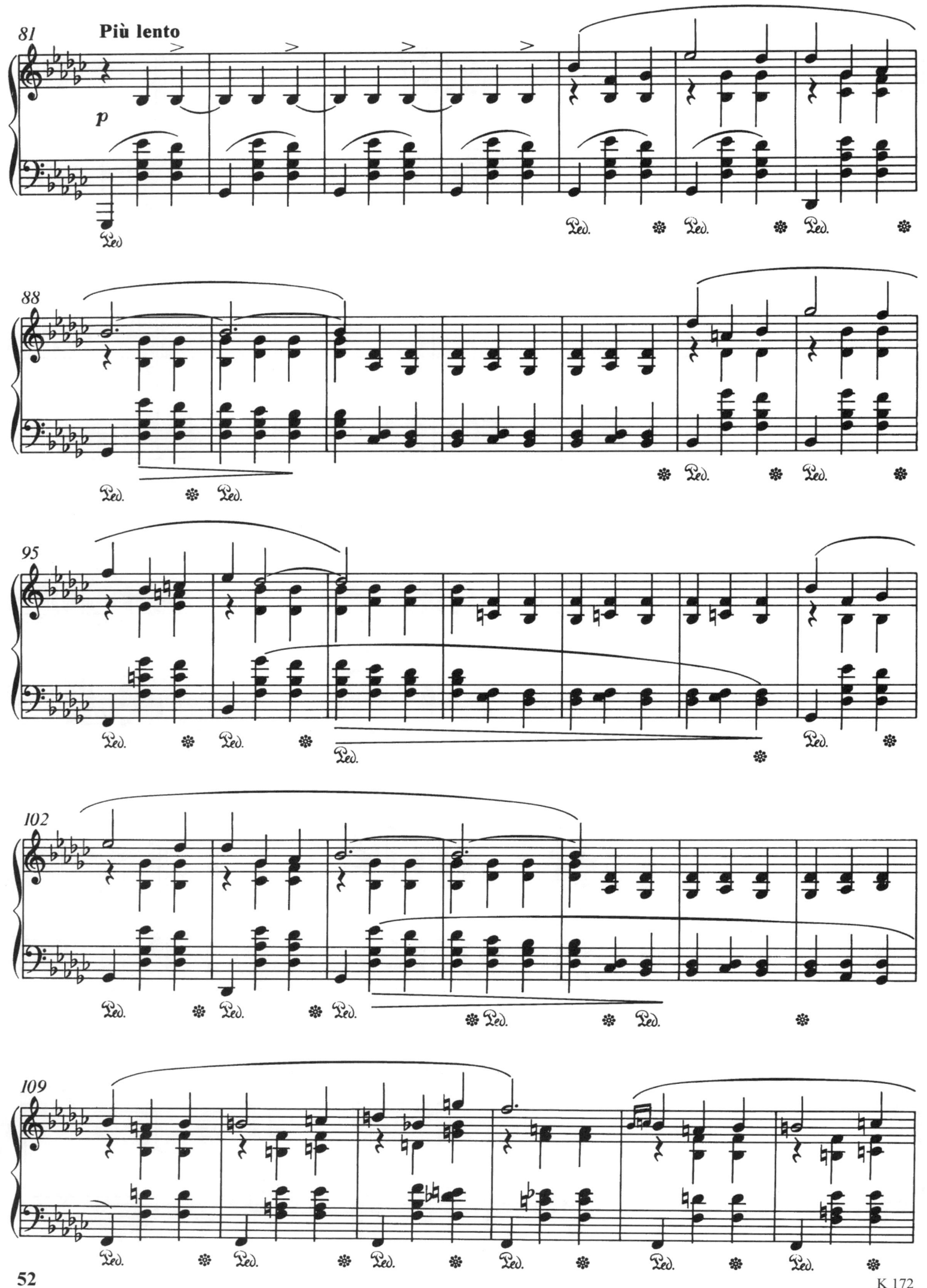

Sonate

Op. 58
Brown-Index 155
1844

Allegro maestoso

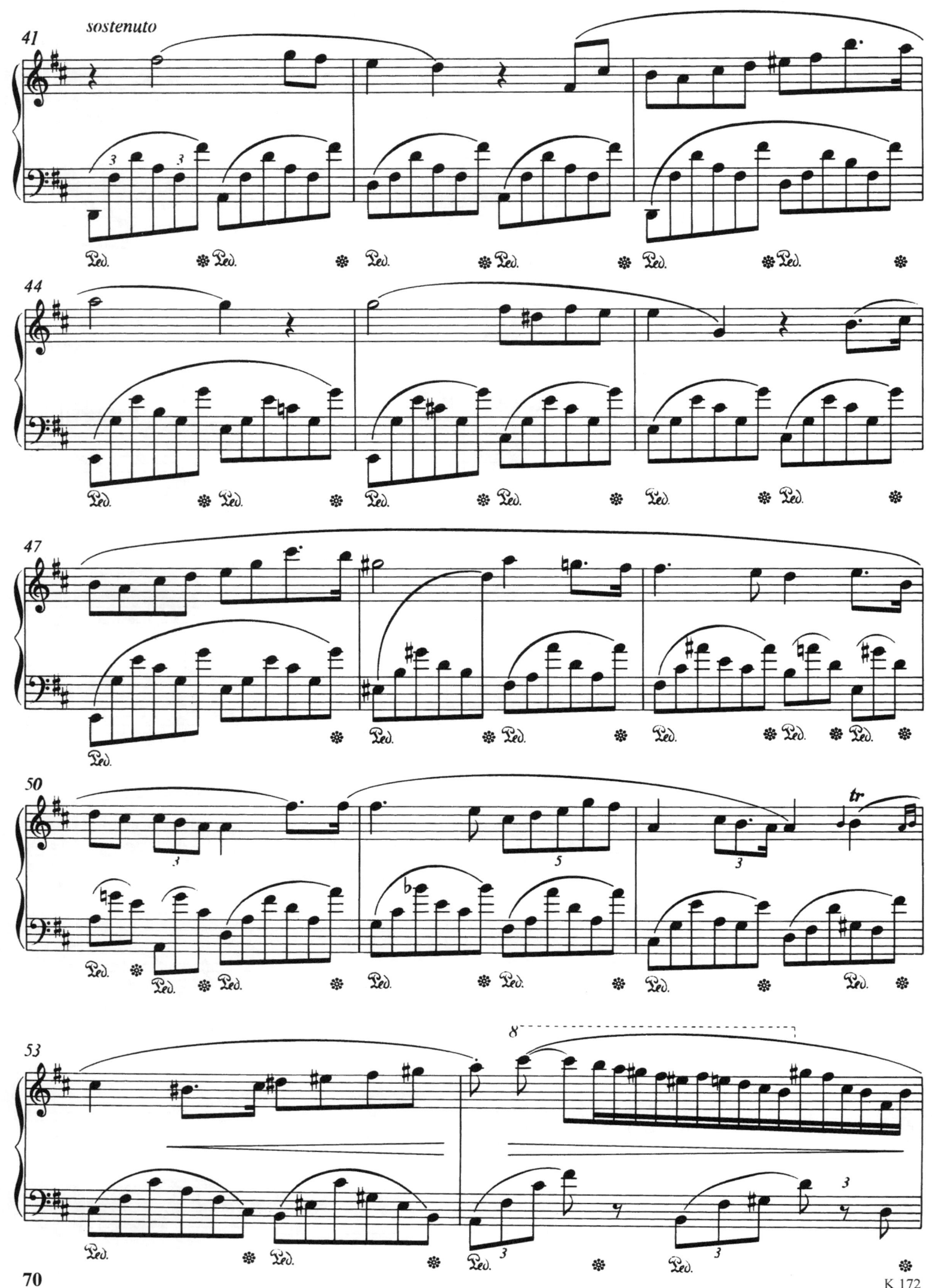

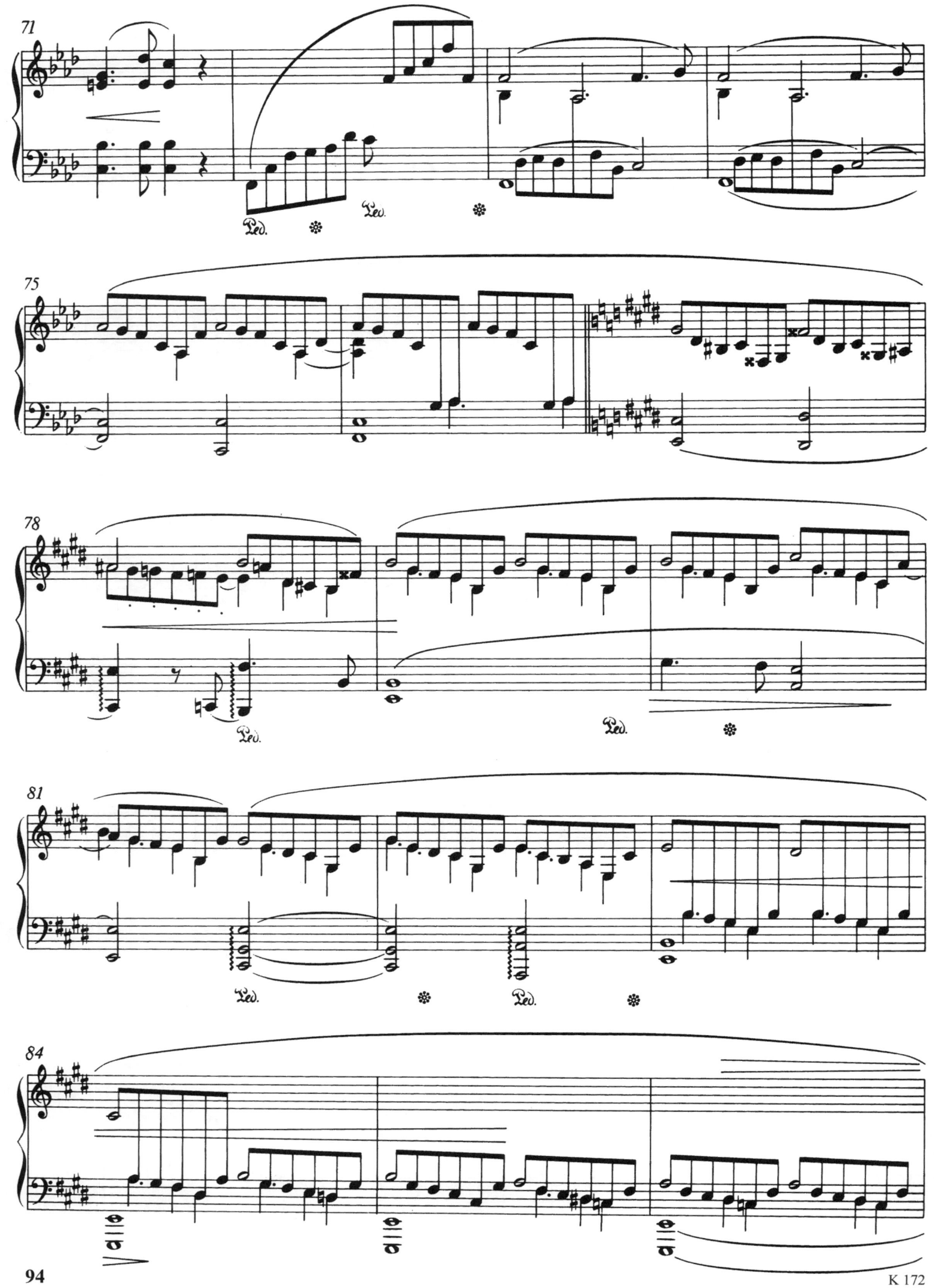